# THE ESSENTIAL
# ELVIS

Susan Doll, Ph.D.

Publications International, Ltd.

**Susan Doll** holds a Ph.D. in radio, television, and film studies from Northwestern University. An instructor of film studies at Oakton Community College and a writer of film and popular culture, she is a sought-after expert on the works and life of Elvis Presley. She has appeared on *The Joan Rivers Show* and National Public Radio to discuss Presley and other topics related to popular film. She is the author of numerous books on popular culture, notably *Elvis: A Tribute to His Life, The Films of Elvis Presley, Marilyn: Her Life and Legend, Elvis: Rock 'n' Roll Legend, Best of Elvis, Understanding Elvis, Elvis: Forever in the Groove, Elvis: American Idol,* and *Florida on Film.*

### ACKNOWLEDGMENTS

The following passages, reprinted by permission, are excerpted from *Elvis Up Close By Those Who Knew Him Best* by Rose Clayton and Dick Heard; Turner Publishing, Atlanta, 1994. Page 6: "I think the very bottom line..." Page 11: We got this boy here..." Page 12: "Man, Elvis just destroyed 'em..." Page 29: "It was bedlam..." Page 30: "It didn't matter..." Page 30: "At Russwood Park..." Page 33: "Elvis loved..." Page 35: "Elvis had to leave..." Page 37: "Early in my association..." Page 55: "I didn't really..." Page 63: "The legendary Elvis scarves..."

### ADDITIONAL COPYRIGHT INFORMATION

"Don't Be Cruel" sheet music cover©1956 Shalimar Music Corp. and Elvis Presley Music, Inc., music and words by Otis Blackwell and Elvis Presley, 17; *Love Me Tender* ©20th Century-Fox Film Corp., 78; "Elvis, An American Trilogy," single ©BMG/RCA Victor, 59; "Heartbreak Hotel" single ©BMG/RCA Victor, 16; "One Broken Heart for Sale," single ©BMG/RCA Victor, 21; *Elv1s 30 #1 Hits,* CD ©BMG/RCA Victor, 76; *Elvis Aloha from Hawaii via Satellite,* album ©BMG/RCA Victor, 21; *Elvis and His Show* poster ©BMG/RCA Victor, 43; *Elvis at Madison Square Garden,* poster ©BMG/RCA Victor, 68; *Elvis Is Back!* ©BMG/RCA Victor, 21, 36; *Elvis Presley* album ©BMG/RCA Victor, 36; *How Great Thou Art,* album ©BMG/RCA Victor, 49; *Elvis on Tour,* documentary ©MGM, 65; *Jailhouse Rock* ©MGM, 26; *Kissin' Cousins* ©MGM, Contents, 44, 45; *G.I. Blues* ©Paramount Pictures Corporation, 60; *King Creole* ©Paramount Pictures Corporation, 32; "Baby Let's Play House" ©Sun Records, 9; "Good Rockin' Tonight" ©Sun Records, 9; "Milkcow Blues Boogie" ©Sun Records, 9; "Mystery Train" ©Sun Records, 9; "That's All Right" ©Sun Records, 9; "Decide Which Elvis Is King" promo ©U.S. Postal Service, Contents, 74; *Dead Elvis: A Chronicle of Cultural Obsession,* by Greil Marcus, 80; *Early Elvis: The Tupelo Years,* by Bill E. Burk, 80; *Elvis and Gladys,* by Elaine Dundy, 80; *Elvis: His Life from A to Z,* by Fred L. Worth and Steve D. Tamerius, 80.

### PHOTO CREDITS:

FRONT COVER: **PIL Collection**
BACK COVER: **Bill E. Burk Collection** (bottom right); **PIL Collection** (top & bottom left).

**Maria Columbus Collection:** 13, 22, 30 (top), 48, 52, 54, 55, 62; **Susan Doll Collection:** 80 (top, top left center & bottom left center; **Sharon Fox Collection:** 5, 17 (top), 18, 21 (center & bottom), 23, 29, 30 (center), 36 (bottom), 40, 43 (top), 47, 50, 63, 65, 67 (left center); **Getty Images:** 24, 25, 41 (left), 51, 69 (top); **Globe Photos:** NBC Photo, 57; **Heavenlea Productions, www.elvispresleynews.com:** 8, 10, 34, 35, 60; **Dwight K. Irwin:** 80 (bottom); **Joseph A. Krein, www.elvis2001.net:** 15, 68, 70, 74, 78; **NASA:** 41 (right); **Personality Photos, Inc.:** Howard Frank, 33; **Photofest:** 53, 67 (top); **PIL Collection:** 9, 16, 17 (bottom), 19, 21 (top), 26, 27, 31, 36 (top), 49, 59, 71, 76; **Ger Rijff Collection:** 7, 11, 28, 30 (bottom), 32, 39, 44, 45, 61, 72; **Rockin' Robin Rosaaen~All The King's Things Collection:** 42, 43 (bottom left), 66, 73; **Showtime Archives:** Colin Escott, 20, 37; **SuperStock:** William Hamilton, 69 (left); Michael Rutherford, 75.

COLORIZING: Cheryl Winser

ADDITIONAL PHOTOGRAPHY: Brian Warling Photography; Sam Griffith Photography; Dave Szarzak/White Eagle Studios.

ISBN-13: 978-1-4127-1493-8
ISBN-10: 1-4127-1493-1

Manufactured in China.

8 7 6 5 4 3 2 1

# Contents

*From left: Elvis on* The Ed Sullivan Show, *in his dual role in*
Kissin' Cousins, *and in a U.S. Postal Service promo.*

# WANT TO TAKE A CRASH COURSE ON
# *Elvis Presley?*

In the time it takes to read *The Essential Elvis,* you will learn enough about the King to understand his significance to popular music and popular history. The key ingredients are all here: the roots of his music, the public storm over his provocative performing style, his important songs and albums, the changes in his career, and the fan phenomenon.

In addition to these high points, the full story of Elvis Presley also involves the flops, the bad movies, the controversies, and the poor decisions that plagued him. You'll learn how these factors affected his music and his career and how they colored popular and critical perceptions of his work. Most importantly, you'll see how these successes and failures combined to propel Elvis into the role of a uniquely American cultural icon—a mythic figure who looms large in the public's consciousness, whether you're a fan or not.

Of course, not every memorable song, quote, or detail could be included in such a compact format. But there's enough here both to inspire the uninitiated to explore the King with more depth and to remind lifelong fans of their favorite songs, movies, and memories.

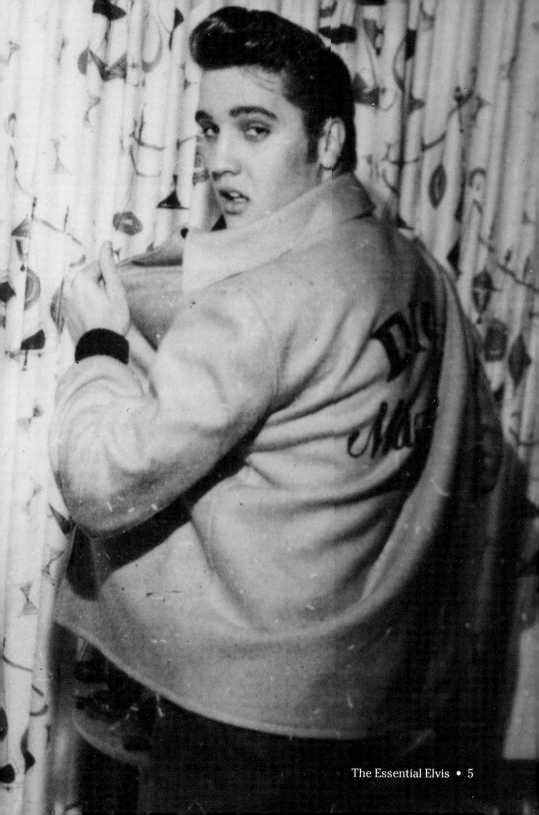

Chapter One

# Rock 'n' Roller (1954–1960)

"I think the very bottom line of rockabilly music was country boys influenced with country music and then Southern black spirituals—maybe not altogether the black spirituals, but that rhythm—that feel—that black music had."

—*Carl Perkins*

## ESSENTIAL SONG
# "That's All Right"

Arguably, the most essential recording of a major singer's career is his or her first release. "That's All Right," backed by "Blue Moon of Kentucky," was Elvis's first recorded song made available to the public. After Elvis recorded "That's All Right" in July 1954, Sun Records, a small, regionally based company, released it that same month.

It was clear from the beginning that Elvis was combining a variety of musical genres—blues, country, and rhythm-and-blues. This was true of his style and also his choice of songs. Blues artist Arthur "Big Boy" Crudup had written and recorded "That's All Right," and the legendary Bill Monroe had written "Blue Moon of Kentucky," which became a bluegrass standard. Elvis's approach to both songs differed from the originals. He used a more relaxed vocal style and higher key for "That's All Right" than Crudup had. He sped up the tempo for "Blue Moon of Kentucky" and omitted the high-pitched bluegrass singing style. Two elements were added to both songs that would make Elvis's sound unique: syncopation and a "slapback" (electronically delayed) echo effect.

Eventually dubbed "rockabilly," Elvis's music for Sun Records became one of the core sounds of rock 'n' roll.

# *Elvis's Recordings on Sun Records*

1. "Good Rockin' Tonight" and "I Don't Care If the Sun Don't Shine"

2. "That's All Right" and "Blue Moon of Kentucky"

3. "Baby Let's Play House" and "I'm Left, You're Right, She's Gone"

4. "Mystery Train" and "I Forgot to Remember to Forget"

5. "Milkcow Blues Boogie" and "You're a Heartbreaker"

# Sam Phillips (1923–2003)

### ELECTED TO ROCK 'N' ROLL HALL OF FAME IN 1986

Raised in Alabama, Sam Phillips was influenced by his rural Southern roots. Around the cotton fields with African-Americans, Phillips was exposed to gospel and blues music. Meanwhile, he experienced the poverty and hard life of many Depression-era Southern families. As a record producer, he would draw on those experiences to shape a new musical aesthetic—a purely Southern

*Sam Phillips and Elvis are at Sun Studio, around 1955–1956.*

sound that combined black rhythm-and-blues and white country western with a hardscrabble philosophy born of bad times. The new music that emerged was a Dixie-fried sound called "rockabilly."

Phillips's genius lay in recognizing the raw talent of regional singers and musicians. These performers often were unaware of their own musical strengths. He worked with these young, inexperienced musicians until they had developed their own sound and personal style. Of his devotion to Southern music, the veteran producer declared, "I just knew this culture, and it was so embedded in these people because of hardship....Generation after generation, these people have been overlooked—black and white."

**"We got this boy here from Humes High School, and this is his first record, and the first time we're playing it. I want to see what y'all like about it."**

—Dewey Phillips, introducing "That's All Right," July 7, 1954. He was the first deejay to play an Elvis record.

## On the Radio
# *Louisiana Hayride*

In mid-October 1954, Elvis performed for the first time on the *Louisiana Hayride*, a radio program broadcast from the Municipal Auditorium in Shreveport, Louisiana. The *Hayride*, unlike the *Grand Ole Opry*, had always encouraged innovative country talent, including Hank Williams, Slim Whitman, Jim Reeves, and Webb Pierce.

Elvis and his band (Scotty Moore and Bill Black) sang "That's All Right" and "Blue Moon of Kentucky" during the "Lucky Strike Guest Time" segment, which was devoted to new artists. The trio was so well received that they were asked to return the next week. On November 6, the *Louisiana Hayride* offered them a one-year contract to perform every weekend. The show paid scale wages, but it gave the trio valuable exposure to fans outside of the Deep South. In doing so, the *Hayride* made an immeasurable contribution to Elvis's career.

---

"Man, Elvis just destroyed 'em on that next performance. They rushed the stage, and I had never seen them rush the stage like that, not even for Hank Williams. They were taking pictures like crazy: Pop! Pop! Pop!"

—*Merle Kilgore, a country singer who saw Elvis on the* Louisiana Hayride

*This photo is of Elvis's final appearance on the* Louisiana Hayride *radio program on December 15, 1956.*

# Colonel Tom Parker (1909–1997)

Colonel Tom Parker met Elvis Presley in 1955, when the singer was under the management of Bob Neal. Parker recognized that Elvis was more than a new singer with a new sound, so he maneuvered himself to be Presley's sole manager by March 1956.

In the story of Elvis's career, Parker is the man everyone loves to hate. Yet, there is no question that he guided his client's career to heights neither could have imagined. He not only controlled Elvis's career but often his image, managing to smooth over criticism on more than one occasion. In 1956, when the controversy over Elvis's "gyrations" escalated in newspapers and magazines, the Colonel distracted the press with stories of "his boy's" close relationship with his parents and generous charity donations. He took advantage of Elvis's time in the army to shape a new image for Presley as a mature, pop-singing movie star who appealed to a broader audience than he had in the 1950s. Indeed, that was the Colonel's goal—to broaden Presley's appeal without losing the core audience of fans.

Critics, however, point to the Colonel's lack of interest in the quality of his client's music and films, which showed his lack of foresight. For example, Parker preferred to tie Elvis to an endless string of three-film deals in musical comedies rather than let his client stretch his acting skills in serious movie dramas.

Parker himself boasted a life story right out of a novel. Born Andreas Cornelius van Kuijk in Breda, Holland, he kept his background in the shadows until after Elvis's death, when his real name came out during a lawsuit. He allegedly entered the United States illegally in 1929 after jumping from a ship docked in Florida. Reasons for leaving his native country vary, though author Alanna Nash claims in her biography of Parker that he fled after killing a woman in a rage.

THE COLONEL

Parker took his dark secrets to the grave on January 21, 1997.

# How Much Does It Cost If It's Free?

*—the title of the Colonel's proposed autobiography,*
*though he never intended to write it*

# "Heartbreak Hotel" vs. "Don't Be Cruel"

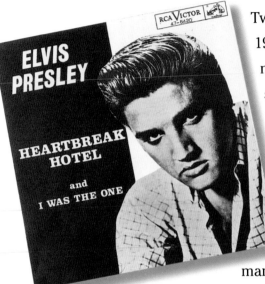

Two of Elvis's biggest hits from 1956—the year he became a national sensation in a mainstream market—reveal two different threads in his musical style.

The lyrics for "Heartbreak Hotel" were inspired by a newspaper story about a businessman who had committed suicide. "I walk a lonely street," read his suicide note, which spurred songwriter Tommy Durden to seek out publicist Mae Axton to cowrite a song about alienation and abject despair. Axton offered the song to Elvis, and Elvis recorded it during his first session with RCA. Elvis rendered the song in a melodramatic style, reminiscent of pop singer Johnnie Ray, famous for his ballad "Cry." But the blues-tinged tone, aided by Scotty Moore's guitar breaks, Floyd Cramer's piano, and the magnified echo effect created a sense of desolation that was raw—like the blues.

"Don't Be Cruel," on the other hand, was influenced by pop music stylings, specifically those of Dean Martin from his 1955

*Elvis poses with R&B singer Jackie Wilson after Wilson performed in Dick Clark's "Good 'Ol Rock 'n' Roll Review" at the Las Vegas Hilton, August 18, 1974. Elvis had been a big fan of Wilson's since the 1950s. When Wilson had a debilitating stroke in 1975, Elvis paid part of his medical expenses.*

hit "Memories Are Made of This." As smooth and fluid as "Hotel" is down and dirty, "Don't Be Cruel" reveals Elvis singing an up-tempo song with the Jordanaires nicely harmonizing as backup. Later, Elvis heard African-American pop singer Jackie Wilson, a

performer he greatly admired, sing "Don't Be Cruel" in Las Vegas. Wilson slowed down the pace, carefully enunciated the syllables of each lyric, and sang the last lines with flourish. Thereafter, Elvis's live performances of "Don't Be Cruel" usually offered a hint of Wilson's interpretation of the song.

# 1956: A Very Good Year

*This colorized publicity photo is of Elvis with a guitar in front of the RCA microphone. The original photo was taken in January 1956 at Elvis's first recording session for RCA. This photo was used to advertise a portable RCA record player that played singles.*

Sam Phillips sold Elvis's contract to nationally based RCA Records in November 1955. Recording for RCA gave Elvis exposure to mainstream audiences and primed him for television appearances on the major variety shows of the period, including *Tommy and Jimmy Dorsey's Stage Show, The Milton Berle Show, The Steve Allen Show,* and *The Ed Sullivan Show.* A television appearance in April attracted the attention of movie producer Hal Wallis, who signed Elvis to a contract. By the end of 1956, Elvis had conquered the major industries of show business— recording, television, and film.

## IN THE NEWS IN 1956

- During the long bus boycott in Montgomery, Alabama, 11 African-Americans are arrested.

- The last Union soldier of the Civil War dies.

- The SS *Andrea Doria* sinks after colliding with another ship.

- The Salk polio vaccine goes on the open market.

- Hungary revolts against Soviet oppression, but their efforts are crushed.

- Dwight David Eisenhower is re-elected president.

- Boston ministers call for the banning of rock 'n' roll; a Connecticut psychiatrist calls rock 'n' roll "a communicable disease."

Sirs:
I hate Elvis Presley!    DANNY ROSE

Rye, N.Y.

Sirs:
The actions of those teenage girls made me realize how silly and simple I was when I almost went haywire over Johnny Ray. I guess it is just a phase we all go through.    JERRY SMITH

Ambler, Pa.

LIFE, SEPTEMBER 17, 1956

## LETTERS To The Editors
### Elvis

Sirs:
I'm an Elvis Presley fan writing to thank you for the nine-page article on him ("Elvis—a Different Kind of Idol." *Life*, August 27). Some time ago you had a short article on him. That was good, but I really flipped when I saw this story.
    JUDY McCLELLAND
White Plains, N.Y.

Sirs:
We want to thank you for that picture spread you had about our "dream baby"—Elvis. It was the "badest," and when I say the "bad-est," "that means the "greatest." The "cats'" here in Philly are wild about Elvis. He's the "king," the supreme ruler.
    STELLA VERBIT
Philadelphia, Pa.

Sirs:
Please don't give the wrong impressions of Elvis Presley. We think he's the absolute end.
    JANIS OLSEN
Grand Junction, Colo.

Sirs:
No one complains about the female strip-teasers, but when it comes to Elvis, it's a different story. When he was on The Milton Berle Show, the criticisms started flying. But when a girl danced the way an uncivilized native would, no one said a thing. That really scorched me.
    CAROL PARKER
Rochester, N.Y.

Sirs:
Few stories featuring Elvis Presley seem to include much about his family or his parents. Could you tell me if he has any brothers or sisters?
    BOBBIE JEAN POLEET
Hanover, Ind.

*No sisters: a twin brother died at birth.—ED.*

# Otis Blackwell (1932–2002)

*Otis Blackwell*

Respected singer-songwriter Otis Blackwell composed many rock 'n' roll standards in the 1950s and 1960s. Born in Brooklyn, Blackwell grew up admiring country-western singer and actor Tex Ritter. He became a staff writer for Shalimar Music in early 1956 after he sold six songs, including "Don't Be Cruel," for $25 each to Shalimar. Blackwell had been standing in front of the Brill Building (home to rock 'n' roll music publishing) in New York City on Christmas Eve when an arranger took him inside to meet Shalimar's owners. They purchased the songs and hired him after the holidays.

Elvis recorded ten Blackwell compositions, including "All Shook Up" and "Return to Sender" (co-written with Winfield Scott). Although Blackwell also sang in Elvis's place on the demos and skillfully imitated his style, he and Elvis never met. After his title song for *Roustabout* was rejected, Blackwell stopped writing for Elvis. Considering his track record, that was arguably a mistake on the part of the decision makers. Among Blackwell's other rock 'n' roll classics are Jerry Lee Lewis's "Great Balls of Fire."

## OTHER SONGS WRITTEN OR CO-WRITTEN BY
# *Otis Blackwell*

"Breathless"

"Fever" (recorded by,
      but not written for, Elvis)

"Handy Man"

"Hey Little Girl"

"Just Keep It Up"

"Make Me Know It"
      (recorded by Elvis)

"One Broken Heart for Sale"
      (recorded by Elvis)

"Paralyzed" (recorded by Elvis)

*Features "Fever"*

*Features "Make Me Know It"*

*Features "One Broken Heart for Sale"*

## ESSENTIAL CITY

# *Jacksonville, Florida*

Jacksonville looms large in Elvis folklore for more than one reason. On May 13, 1955, Elvis performed at the Gator Bowl in front of 14,000 people, along with *Grand Ole Opry* stars Hank Snow, Faron Young, and members of the Carter Family. Since the girls in the audience were enthusiastic as usual, Elvis joked at the end of his set, "I'll see all you girls backstage." The girls took him at his word and pushed en masse through a gate that was accidentally left ajar. When they found him, they tore his pink shirt completely off his body, stole his shoes as he tried to escape to a shower stall, and

*Elvis did six shows at the Florida Theater in Jacksonville, August 10–11, 1956. Judge Marion W. Gooding attended the first show and forced Elvis to tone down his act.*

*Elvis is in Jacksonville, Florida, in August 1956 on a date with a fan who won the "Win a Date with Elvis" contest from* Hit Parader *teenzine.*

went for his pants. Young and songwriter Mae Axton, among others, rescued him. Headlines blared, "Girls Tear Clothes Off Elvis Presley," which influenced teenage girls everywhere to mob Elvis after his performances. The incident marked a turning point for Elvis in understanding both the positive and negative sides of fame.

The following year, on August 10, Elvis was ordered to "quieten his act" by Judge Marion W. Gooding while in Jacksonville. The order was in response to the criticisms of the singer's energetic performing style in which he gyrated his hips, thrust them forward, and then shook his body, which in turn provoked the girls into hysterics. Understanding the ridiculousness of the order, Elvis wiggled only his little finger during most of his shows. Once again, however, the publicity over the event made it a key moment in his career, because it added more fuel to the controversy over his performing style.

# Berle vs. Allen

*Elvis sings "Hound Dog" to an admirer on* The Steve Allen Show.

The television appearance that generated the most controversy was when Elvis appeared on *The Milton Berle Show* on June 5, 1956. His highly charged performance of "Hound Dog" had spurred more commotion than any other single event in Elvis's career. For the climax of "Hound Dog," Elvis slowed down the tempo to repeat the song's chorus. While belting out this final verse to a blues beat, he turned his body in profile and thrust his pelvis at the microphone. Elvis rested his hand next to the crotch of his pants, which emphasized the provocative connotation of the movement.

After the Berle show, Colonel Parker booked Elvis on *The Steve Allen Show,* a new comedy-variety program hungry for good ratings. Though Allen knew about the controversy generated by Elvis, he was also aware of the through-the-roof ratings. The savvy comedian diffused Elvis's sensuality by making him part of the comedy of the show. Elvis's appearance in a tuxedo singing to a sad-eyed basset hound plopped down on a pedestal is almost as famous as his notorious performance on Berle's program.

# The Ed Sullivan Show

No TV appearance has contributed so much to the Elvis Presley legend as *The Ed Sullivan Show,* primarily because of the decision to show Elvis only from the waistup during a performance of "Heartbreak Hotel" and "Hound Dog." Even nonfans know this tidbit of Elvis lore. Much, however, has been exaggerated about the event. The truth is that the order came during Elvis's *third* appearance on Sullivan's show. How much Sullivan had to do with the decision is unknown.

## Let's Dance
# "*Jailhouse Rock*"

Elvis's performance of the title song from his third film is so iconic that it is seldom discussed from a fresh angle. It is a potent symbol of Elvis in the prime of his early career as a rockin' rebel raging against the chains of the system. Again, folklore colors many of the facts surrounding this performance.

For decades, books claimed that Elvis himself choreographed the dance, but that isn't an accurate account of what happened. It was choreographer Alex Romero who was in charge of the big production number for "Jailhouse Rock." At first, he worked out

*Elvis is having a blast during the shooting of "Jailhouse Rock." The film was released on November 8, 1957.*

some traditional dance steps for Elvis along the lines of Gene Kelly, but it quickly became apparent that these did not suit the young rocker's style. Romero then asked Elvis to play a few of his records and move naturally to them. After studying Elvis's performing style, the choreographer went home and worked out a different routine based on Presley's pelvic gyrations, knee jerks, and other signature moves. The next day, he and Elvis rehearsed the new dance, which the singer quickly picked up. Elvis may have contributed to this well-known production number, but he did not choreograph it.

The set for the number was a simple scaffolding with barred doors; it was so minimalist that it was almost abstract, which differed from the more naturalistic settings of most of his production numbers throughout his film career. The result is a more timeless look to the set design, compared to the time-bound nature of most of his movie musical numbers.

# Scotty, Bill, and D. J.

*Scotty Moore, Elvis, and Bill Black were the Hillbilly Cat and the Blue Moon Boys in 1955.*

Elvis, guitarist Scotty Moore, and bass player Bill Black were dubbed the Hillbilly Cat and the Blue Moon Boys back in 1954. Moore and Black had hitched their wagons to Elvis's star after recording "That's All Right" with him. Moore's driving guitar sound helped create Elvis's style, while Black's antics on his upright bass added humor and excitement to their live act. Later, drummer D. J. Fontana joined the group on the road, although he never played on any of Elvis's Sun recordings.

After Elvis became a household name, Moore, Black, and Fontana were not given the respect and salary they were due. Moore and Black split with Elvis in September 1957 over this issue. Both were wooed back, but the relationship among the three was never the same. Moore and Fontana recorded with Elvis after he returned from the army in 1960, but Black had already struck out on his own, enjoying moderate success with his own combo.

*"It was bedlam onstage. The noise was so loud we couldn't hear him play; we had to watch him. D. J. [Fontana], being an old burlesque drummer, could follow Elvis and take cues from his body motions and get us through it."*

—*Scotty Moore*

*From left are D. J. Fontana, Scotty Moore, Bill Black, and Elvis. They are poolside at the New Frontier Hotel in Las Vegas, April 1956.*

# Elvis and the Girls

"It didn't matter what he did [onstage]. He would act silly or say something silly—get the words wrong or make up words. He just couldn't do anything wrong....I learned since—it was because he really loved his audience. He loved his fans more than anybody I've ever seen."

—*Wanda Jackson, country singer*

"At Russwood Park, Elvis was the primary entertainer. . . . The girls threw apartment keys to him. I'm not lying to you. They were screaming, and they would actually pull out their own hair."

—*Bill Perry, Elvis's neighbor in Lauderdale Courts*

# The Gold Lamé Suit

Hollywood clothing designer Nudie Cohen created the famous gold suit for Elvis for his 1957 tour. The suit consisted of gold lamé slacks and a jacket woven from spun gold thread, but Elvis disliked it because it was heavy and uncomfortable. The pants ripped during the tour, and Elvis never wore the entire suit again, though he does appear in full lamé splendor on the cover of the 1959 album *50,000,000 Elvis Fans Can't Be Wrong: Elvis' Gold Records, Vol. 2.* The suit is so well known that it has become an icon of the King's early years, and it was lampooned by rival Pat Boone on a 1964 album cover.

# King Creole

A musical drama with a cast of Hollywood's most respected character actors, *King Creole* was directed by veteran Michael Curtiz and produced by Hal Wallis for Paramount Pictures. Though not a classic, it is a well-crafted example of a typical Hollywood film from the era when the studio system still dominated the industry.

*In* King Creole *(1958), Walter Matthau plays tough guy Maxie Fields, and Elvis plays rebellious teenager Danny Fisher.*

The film was adapted for Elvis's specific image and talents but not at the expense of the drama, characters, or setting. Rich in the atmosphere of old New Orleans, *King Creole* seems authentic and believable, unlike some of his later musical vehicles. The film benefited from the performances of a stellar cast that included Walter Matthau, Carolyn Jones, Vic Morrow, Dean Jagger, and Paul Stewart. Elvis held his own among these talented professionals, and *King Creole* stands as testament to his acting potential, which was never fully realized.

*Elvis struggles with Shark, played by Vic Morrow.*

"Elvis loved King Creole because it was more of a dramatic role, even though it did have songs in it. He said he was very pleased with it. He liked the fact that he had the chance to act a little bit."

*—Arlene Cogan Bradley, part of Elvis's gang of Hollywood friends during the 1950s*

## No Place Like Home
# *1034 Audubon Drive*

*Vernon and Gladys Presley stand in the carport of the Presleys' home at 1034 Audubon Drive, Memphis. Elvis bought the house in May 1956 and lived there until he bought Graceland.*

In May 1956, Elvis purchased a pale green-and-white ranch-style house located in a nice suburb of Memphis. This became the first home that the Presleys owned outright. For his $40,000, Elvis got a modern single-story, three-bedroom house, which he improved with a swimming pool in the backyard. It did not take long for fans to track him down. He sometimes spent hours in the driveway signing autographs. His mother, Gladys, occasionally sent cold water or iced tea to the fans if they had been standing in the hot sun for very long. Less than a year later, Elvis purchased Graceland and moved his family to a more private location.

In 2006, the Audubon Drive house made the news in a bizarre story that proves truth is stranger than fiction. The owners decided to auction off the house on eBay, speculating that the Elvis connection would generate a high price. Minutes before the auction closed on May 14, renowned psychic Uri Geller bid $905,000, which was accepted by the owners. Geller, who claims he has a paranormal connection to the number 11, told the press, "...I felt intuitively I got the price. I was text-messaging Gleason [his financial partner] and it was exactly 11 on my mobile phone and suddenly the radio was playing an Elvis song. That was Elvis telling me we had got the house."

Unfortunately for Geller, he misread Elvis's "message," because the sale was never finalized; the house was then sold to Mike Curb, former owner of Curb Records, for a cool million. Curb donated the use of the house to Memphis' Rhodes College as part of his Curb Institute of Music, though he retained ownership.

*This publicity photo was released to teenzines and fanzines in 1956.*

*"Elvis had to leave Audubon Drive because of the fans. The other people who lived on the street got up a petition to get him to move because fans and other people's cars were there day and night—going up and down the street—honking. Guys would be yelling, 'Elvis, do you have any extra girlfriends?'"*

*—Barbara Glidewell, friend from the 1950s*

# Elvis Presley vs. Elvis Is Back!

*Elvis Presley* was the singer's first album, which was released by RCA Records, not Sun. Moving to RCA meant going national and international in promotion and distribution. Steve Sholes, RCA's premier A&R (artist and repertoire) man, had helped sign Elvis, and he was aware that the execs were closely watching this unusual new artist who did not fit into any of the company's existing categories of music. Elvis did not read music, nor did he have any professional experience arranging it. He had an instinctive approach to recording, in which he sang, played it back, discarded it, and then sang another. Thus, Sholes watched Elvis during his first recording session on January 10 and 11, 1956, with some trepidation.

But Sholes and RCA need not have worried, because *Elvis Presley* sold more than 360,000 copies in about six weeks. The career of RCA's most famous artist was launched.

*Elvis Is Back!* was the singer's first album after his two-year stint in the army, and the popular music scene had changed a great deal since 1958. Smooth-sounding teen angels such as Bobby Vee and Frankie Avalon romanced listeners on the radio, while a dance craze called the Twist propelled them across the dance floor. Elvis and the Colonel remolded his image around current trends and away from the rock 'n' roll controversy that had followed him into the army. *Elvis Is Back!* offered an eclectic collection of musical genres, from a sentimental duet with Charlie Hodge called "I Will Be Home Again" to the gritty "Reconsider Baby." Once again, Elvis's talent of unifying disparate styles of music resulted in a creative album, which restarted his recording career and reached number two on the charts.

*"Early in my association with RCA, I worked for Steve Sholes. Steve felt Elvis was going to be a tremendous star, and, you know, the feeling of the other people at RCA was not all that enthusiastic. There were an awful lot of brass at RCA who felt Elvis was going to be a flash in the pan."*

Steve Sholes and Elvis

—*Joan Deary, former assistant to Steve Sholes*

## Chapter Two

# Movie Star (1960–1969)

"A Presley picture is the only sure thing in Hollywood."

*—Hal Wallis, the first producer to sign Elvis to a film contract*

# A Very Good Year

## 1960

Elvis's ducktail haircut, 1956.

Elvis returned from the army in March 1960 ready to resume his career. He recorded and released an album in just over a month; appeared on Frank Sinatra's television special; and starred in a new movie, *G.I. Blues*, before the year was out. Aside from the ease with which he returned to his career, 1960 marked a new maturity for Elvis and a deliberate change in his star status.

Elvis's image as a notorious rock 'n' roll singer had all but disappeared by the time he was discharged from the army. A different image was constructed and circulated to replace it—one that was neither controversial nor dangerous. Presley's management team, particularly Colonel Parker, developed the new image to shift Presley away from rock 'n' roll music and to attract the mainstream audience—the latter being Parker's goal for Presley since their association began.

Elvis's more conservative hair style, 1962

As the year progressed, Elvis pursued his film career as a leading man, refrained from making controversial remarks to the press, and fostered a mature look with a more conservative haircut and trimmed sideburns. Essential to understanding Elvis's career is appreciating this change as a successful attempt to appeal to a mainstream audience—not as a decline in music or movies.

## IN THE NEWS IN 1960

- Fidel Castro signs an economic agreement with Russia.

- The Civil Rights Act provides voting guarantees.

*John F. Kennedy*

- John F. Kennedy is elected president.

- The world's first weather satellite, *Tiros I,* and first communications satellite, *Echo I,* are launched.

- The first brand of birth control pills is marketed.

- Motown Records is born.

Echo 1

# ESSENTIAL CITY

## *Honolulu*

One of Elvis's favorite locations was the Hawaiian islands. Three of his films were made there, *Girls! Girls! Girls!, Blue Hawaii,* and *Paradise, Hawaiian Style.* The islands' capital city, Honolulu, benefited from Presley's generosity on more than one occasion.

*Elvis arrives at the Honolulu Airport on January 9, 1973, for his engagement at the Honolulu International Center Arena five days later.*

On March 25, 1961, he gave a benefit concert for the USS *Arizona* Memorial Fund, making it his last public performance until 1969. The concert occurred at Honolulu's Bloch Arena before 4,000 excited fans. The benefit raised more than $62,000 for the memorial to the *Arizona,* which had been sunk during the Japanese attack on Pearl Harbor.

On January 14, 1973, Elvis performed before 6,000 people at Honolulu's International Center Arena. The concert became the first to be telecast worldwide. More than 1 billion people in 40 countries saw Elvis's concert, dubbed *Aloha from Hawaii.* The concert was a benefit for the Kuiokalani (Kui) Lee Cancer Fund.

*This program was for Elvis's concert at Bloch Arena in Honolulu on March 25, 1961. Elvis performed a benefit at Pearl Harbor to raise money for a memorial for the USS Arizona.*

## ESSENTIAL MOVIE
# Kissin' Cousins

*Kissin' Cousins* is often considered the beginning of the end of Elvis's film career, largely because Sam Katzman, who was known for his cheaply made movies, produced it.

In the mid-1960s, well-respected Hollywood producer Hal Wallis, who had brought Elvis to Hollywood in 1956, decided not to renew his contract. The Colonel was forced to find other producers to finance his client's movies. Since Elvis's movies made less money at the box office, the Colonel wanted someone who could work with lower budgets. Parker signed a deal with producer Sam Katzman to make two films, *Harum Scarum* and *Kissin' Cousins.* Katzman had earned the nickname "King of the Quickies" because he made films quickly for very little money by cutting corners. Each of the films

*In this dance number with Cynthia Pepper (left) and Yvonne Craig (right) in Kissin' Cousins, which used trick photography, Elvis appears in a dual role as Jodie Tatum and Josh Morgan.*

that Elvis made for Katzman was shot within three weeks, and the production values for each film were weak.

From left: Jack Albertson, Pamela Austin, and Yvonne Craig star in Kissin' Cousins with Elvis.

*Kissin' Cousins* features Elvis in a dual role as soldier Josh Morgan and his country cousin Jodie Tatum. The setting is the mountains of Tennessee, and the film features every backwoods cliché one can imagine—hound dogs, moonshine, oversexed and underdressed country gals, and gun-toting mountain Romeos. Though unintentional, the stereotypes are an insult to Elvis and his rural southern roots. The second-rate songs also have no connection to southern music but are some Hollywood hack's idea of country music.

Though the Colonel moved on to make deals with other producers and studios, the Katzman films represent a creative low point.

# "I'd like to make one good film before I leave. I know this town's laughing at me."

—*Elvis to Marlyn Mason on the set of* The Trouble with Girls

# No Place Like Home
## California

Elvis owned several houses in California, where he spent a fair amount of time in the 1960s. None of these homes ever achieved the mythic status of Graceland or the shotgun shack that was his birthplace in Tupelo, but some of the houses are interesting in their own right.

In 1961, Elvis rented a house at 565 Perugia Way in Bel Air. Originally called the Healy House, this residence was designed by Lloyd Wright in 1949 in the Southern California style. Wright was the son of famed architect Frank Lloyd Wright, and the house is often erroneously attributed to the elder Wright. It was once owned by the Shah of Iran and by movie star Rita Hayworth when she was married to Ali Khan. Elvis lived there from 1961 to mid-1963, then from late 1963 to late 1965.

The only house that Elvis ever built for himself was located at 825 Chino Road in Palm Springs. Built in 1965, this single-story, Spanish-style, white stucco house was set on two acres of land surrounded by a fence. With 15 rooms and a swimming pool, the house was luxurious if not ostentatious. Elvis willed the house to daughter Lisa Marie, but she did not keep it. Among its owners was singer Frankie Valli.

*Snapshot of Elvis and Priscilla in Palm Springs in the late 1960s.*

# How Great Thou Art

From January 1964 to May 1966, Elvis recorded nothing but movie sound tracks, mostly in Hollywood. Dissatisfied with his life because of complex professional and personal reasons, he did not venture into the Nashville studios to cut album material. When he did decide to record new material, he returned to the studio with new musicians and a new producer, Felton Jarvis.

Felton Jarvis produced Elvis's albums, taking over in 1966. He steered Elvis toward better material. Jarvis died in 1981.

Elvis went to RCA studios in Nashville in spring of 1966 to record a gospel album, *How Great Thou Art.* As a child of the South, he was steeped in gospel music, and he especially liked the four-part harmony style sung by male gospel quartets associated with the shape-note singing schools from the early 20th century. Elvis's favorite gospel quartets included the Blackwood Brothers, whom he knew personally, and the Statesmen, whose lead singer had been the colorful Jake Hess. Elvis asked Hess and his new group, the Imperials, to join him.

*How Great Thou Art* proved to be a milestone in Elvis's career, winning him the first of three Grammy Awards, this one for Best Sacred Performance.

"Gospel music is the purest
thing there is on this earth."

—*Elvis*

# A VERY GOOD YEAR

## 1968

Elvis seemed poised for a change in 1968 when he began work on what was supposed to be a televised Christmas special. Producers Steve Binder and Bob Finkel, however, quickly persuaded the singer to abandon the Christmas theme and take a chance on an innovative concept show. The producers wanted the special to

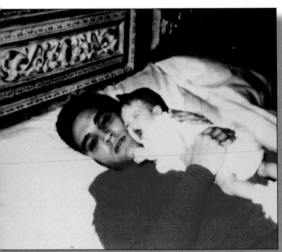

center on Elvis's music and its place in popular culture. Nothing like it had ever been attempted on television, and Elvis was thrilled at the chance to be musically creative again. It inspired him to take his career in a different direction, and after he fulfilled his contractual obligations in Hollywood, he stopped making the movies that he detested. When the special was aired

*Elvis and newborn Lisa Marie rest at home at Graceland in February 1968.*

in December, and the sound track released to the public, Elvis reestablished himself as a musical force.

Commonly called *The '68-Comeback Special,* the show often overshadows other Elvis highlights of the year, which collectively indicate his career had not sunk as low as critics claim. In February, Elvis was elected to *Playboy* magazine's Music Hall of

Fame; in March, his gospel album *How Great Thou Art* was certified gold; and in December, England's *New Musical Express* poll named him Outstanding Male Singer of the year.

Even more significant in 1968 was the birth of his daughter Lisa Marie on February 1, a high point of his personal life.

## IN THE NEWS IN 1968

- The Vietnam War intensifies when the Viet Cong begin the Tet Offensive in Saigon, Hue, and other cities.

- Martin Luther King, Jr., is assassinated in Memphis, Elvis's hometown.

*Martin Luther King, Jr.*

- Robert F. Kennedy is assassinated in Los Angeles, where Elvis has a second home.

- There are major riots in Chicago at the Democratic National Convention.

- Richard M. Nixon is elected president.

- The musical *Hair* begins Off–Broadway.

Hair *the musical*

# The '68 Comeback Special

Producer Steve Binder had a specific vision for his television special with Elvis Presley. He hoped to capture what he felt was Elvis's genius—the adaptation of rhythm-and-blues to the tastes of mainstream audiences. He wanted to prove that Elvis was not a relic of the past but the beginning of a musical revolution that was still underway in 1968.

Originally titled *Elvis,* the special aired December 3, 1968, and was sponsored by Singer Sewing Machines. The special was designed as a concept show, meaning there were no guests, no show-biz chatter, and no comedy skits. All of the segments were designed to showcase Elvis's music—its roots, its influences, and the power behind his live performances.

One segment featured Elvis in a gold lamé jacket while performing "Trouble." The jacket echoed his famous lamé suit from

*Elvis with the creative team behind his 1968 TV special,* Singer Presents Elvis *(later called* The '68 Comeback Special*). From second left: producer Bones Howe, director Steve Binder, Elvis and executive producer Bob Finkel.*

*Elvis performs on* The '68 Comeback Special.

1958 without exactly duplicating it. That approach—reminding viewers of the pre-movie Elvis without making him a carbon copy of the past—was the approach of the entire special. The most famous part of the special was the concert segment, in which Elvis and four musicians sat on a small stage and reminisced about the past while performing updated versions of his hits. Two of those musicians were Scotty Moore and D. J. Fontana, two thirds of the Blue Moon Boys from his 1950s band.

The special received a 32-rating and a 42-share, making it the highest-rated program during the week that it was broadcast. Executive producer Bob Finkel won a Peabody Award for his work on *Elvis.*

# Chips Moman

Invigorated by the success of his television special, Elvis walked through the
door of tiny American Sound Studio
in Memphis in January 1969 to make
quality music that would garner him hit
records. Elvis had not recorded in his
hometown since he left Sun in 1955, but
friends and associates encouraged him
to record at American Sound, a small
studio in a run-down Memphis neigh-
borhood operated by Chips Moman.

*Chips Moman*

Born in LaGrange, Georgia, Moman made his name as one
of the architects of the Memphis Sound, an edgier style of soul
music descended from Memphis's blues and rhythm-and-blues. He
helped establish soulful Stax Records in 1958, and then six years
later, founded American Sound Studios. He occasionally wrote
songs, including the gritty "Dark End of the Street," recorded by
Percy Sledge, Linda Ronstadt, and Roy Hamilton. Moman's talent
as a producer was finding the right material for the right artist. He
produced music for such diverse performers as Wilson Pickett,
Dusty Springfield, B. J. Thomas, Neil Diamond, and the Box Tops.
With Moman as producer, Elvis recorded his first significant mainstream album in years, *From Elvis in Memphis,* in 1969.

*Elvis recorded* From Elvis in Memphis *at American Sound Studio in 1969. The musicians included: (from left) Bobby Wood, Mike Leech, Tommy Cogbill, Gene Chrisman, Elvis, Bobby Emmons, Reggie Young, Ed Kollis, and Dan Penn.*

During the 1970s, Moman and some of his house band began recording in Atlanta, and then he and most of his band moved to Nashville, where he stayed until the 1980s. He produced and played on records by Willie Nelson, Merle Haggard, and Tammy Wynette, among others.

*"I didn't really think anything so special about getting the chance to record Elvis—not when it happened . . . we were so busy producing records. . . . Later I thought to myself, 'It sure was a privilege to have worked with him.' I wish I had realized that at the time we were recording, 'cause there's a lot of things I would have liked to have said to him."*

*—Chips Moman*

Chapter Three

# The Legend (1970 and Beyond)

"It's rare when an artist's talent can touch an entire generation of people. It's even rarer when that same influence affects several generations. Elvis made an imprint on the world of pop music unequaled by any other single performer."

—*Dick Clark*

# "Suspicious Minds" and "An American Trilogy"

These two key songs from the concert era of Elvis's career are good examples of his large-scale musical style that defined his later career. Loud, emotional, even melodramatic, this sound nonetheless embodied an aspect of Elvis's music that went back to his early days (movie sound tracks excluded). That is, it was based on the combination, or integration, of diverse types of music that was reworked until it became uniquely Elvis's style. Who else could sing Sinatra's "My Way," Simon and Garfunkel's "Bridge Over Troubled Water," and Willie Nelson's "Always on My Mind" in the same concert and still call them his own?

Recorded at American Sound Studio, "Suspicious Minds" was Elvis's last number-one single, and at 4 minutes and 22 seconds, it was his longest. It featured backing vocals by Jeannie Green and Ronnie Milsap, a singer-songwriter who later became a country music star. Memphis singer Mark James wrote, recorded, and released "Suspicious Minds," but his version flopped. Chips Moman then brought James's song to Elvis, who loved it. Elvis was convinced that he could turn the song into a hit. Released as a single in September 1969, Elvis's version reached number one in seven weeks.

"An American Trilogy," arranged by country music performer Mickey Newbury, is a medley of "Dixie," "The Battle Hymn of the

Republic," and "All My Trials." Northern reviewers and audiences could never fully grasp the significance of this unusual number, but with its combination of two Civil War-era songs (one Southern and the other Northern) with a traditional spiritual, it is the very essence of Elvis's music in general—the integration of diverse cultural elements.

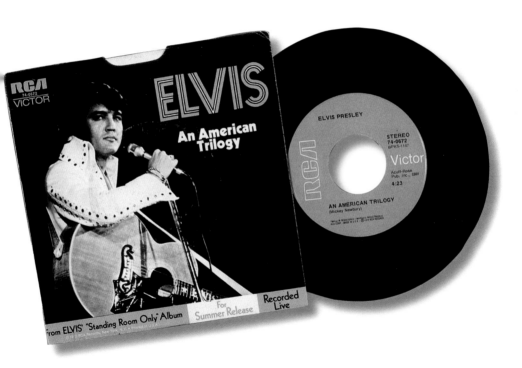

# *Kung Fu Fighting*

**Top:** *Elvis demonstrates karate on the set of* G.I. Blues *(1960).*
**Above:** *During the early 1970s, Elvis devoted his spare time to martial arts competitions.*

It's no secret that Elvis practiced martial arts, particularly karate. Introduced to it while serving in the army in Germany, by 1960, he earned a black belt. By the time he died in 1977, he was an eighth-degree black belt. He also studied Tae Kwon Do with Kang Rhee and Kempo with Ed Parker. Elvis incorporated karate into other parts of his life. He used it in several films, including *G.I. Blues, Follow That Dream,* and *Harum Scarum.*

The rest of the country caught up to Elvis's interest during the 1970s when a martial arts craze swept popular culture. One of Elvis's favorite TV programs was *Kung Fu,* which caught the nation's attention and ran from 1972 to 1975. During his concerts, when Elvis was particularly caught up in the music, he broke into martial arts stances and moves to the delight of the audiences.

Elvis breaks into a martial arts move during a concert from his 1972 fall tour.

*"[Martial arts] is not just self defense, it's about... self control, body discipline, mind discipline... and breathing techniques. It involves yoga. It involves meditation. It's an art, not a sport."*

—*Elvis*

# Las Vegas

This marquee promoted Elvis's engagement at the Las Vegas Hilton. Elvis played the Hilton about two times a year from 1969 to 1976.

Energized by the positive reception to *The '68 Comeback Special,* Elvis Presley decided to return to performing live. In the summer of 1969, he chose the International Hotel in Las Vegas to test the waters. The engagement was arguably his most critically acclaimed and literally set the stage for the last phase of his career. The show set a Las Vegas record of 101,509 paying customers who generated a gross take of $1.5 million. For the rest of his life, Elvis alternated Vegas engagements with extensive touring.

During the 1970s, Vegas was filled with a variety of celebrities who kept a high profile in the hotels they performed in, including the Flamingo (the original Vegas hotel), the Sands, the Stardust, and the Hilton. (The International became the Las Vegas Hilton in 1971 after Barron Hilton purchased it.) Gaudy, garish, and ablaze with lights that lit up the night sky as if it were noon, Vegas was the original "city that never sleeps."

In the 1980s and 1990s, the city re-invented itself as a family destination—with gambling. All of the old hotels were torn down to make way for family-friendly theme-park-style complexes that looked liked parodies of European cities. Despite this makeover of Las Vegas, the Hilton has survived. A large statue of Elvis stands inside the casino entrance near the main showroom to commemorate his contributions to the hotel. Dedicated in 1978, the 400-pound statue is made of bronze. In a nearby glass case lie one of Elvis's guitars and one of his jumpsuits.

*Elvis is in his "Black Phoenix" jumpsuit, which he wore during a 1974 concert.*

*"The legendary Elvis scarves began when we went to Vegas.... He said, 'Why don't you start making me some scarves because I perspire so much, and I can wipe off my face and hand them out to the audience.' He started throwing them out to the fans, and that became a big thing. So I made tons and tons of different colored scarves that I would ship off to him."*

—*Bill Belew, costume designer*

# Denis Sanders, Pierre Adidge, and Robert Abel

Arguably, Elvis's two best films were not narrative features but documentaries. *Elvis: That's the Way It Is* (1970) chronicled his 1970 summer appearance at the International Hotel in Las Vegas, beginning with rehearsals in Hollywood. Director Denis Sanders recorded rehearsals, opening night, and several other performances throughout the engagement, including one show at Veterans Memorial Coliseum in Phoenix. He structured the film so that the rehearsals and other scenes of preparation built to an extended climax of Elvis onstage. Fit, energetic, and handsome, Elvis is captured forever at the pinnacle of his career.

*Elvis on Tour* followed the singer on the road during a 15-city tour in the spring of 1972. The tour started in Buffalo, New York, and came to a rousing conclusion in Albuquerque, New Mexico. The footage of the performer onstage is exhilarating. Filmmakers Pierre Adidge and Robert Abel also attempted to reveal the real Elvis Presley backstage and off guard. A camera recorded the singer and his entourage as Elvis was questioned about his music and childhood. Despite a few humorous candid moments, however, these interviews did not reveal Elvis at all but only added to his legend. The well-shot film won a Golden Globe as Best Documentary of 1972, dispelling the critics' notion that no Elvis film could ever win an award.

*This photo was used for the poster for the documentary* Elvis on Tour *(1972).*

# MYTH MAKER
## *Richard Nixon*

In December 1970, Elvis made a spontane-
ous decision to travel to Washington, D.C.,
to visit Deputy U.S. Narcotics Director
John Finlator. Although Elvis said that he
was going to volunteer his help in the anti-
drug campaign, he was actually hoping to
obtain a federal narcotics badge to add to
his badge collection. Finlator turned down
Elvis's request for a badge, but the King
went over his head. With a couple of his bodyguards, Elvis made
a call on the White House to see President Richard Nixon. As it
turned out, Nixon aide Bud Krogh was a fan and cleared the president's schedule. In a matter of minutes, the charismatic Presley
was able to talk Nixon into giving him an authentic narcotic's
agent badge.

A photo was taken of Elvis shaking hands with Nixon to
commemorate the occasion, and this photo has since become
an icon of the 1970s—often painted as an era of excess and
extravagance—and has graced postcards, t-shirts, watches, and
mugs. In 2007, the Richard Nixon Presidential Library & Birthplace
organized an exhibit of the relics related to this mythic moment
from another place and time.

On December 21, 1970, Elvis visited President Richard Nixon at the White House, where he secured a badge from the Bureau of Narcotics and Dangerous Drugs.

*"Elvis was so happy, he goes over and grabs [Nixon]. One of my abiding memories is Elvis Presley hugging Nixon who's sort of looking up, thinking, 'Oh my god.'"*

—Bud Krogh, former White House aide

# A VERY GOOD YEAR

# *1972*

In addition to the critically acclaimed documentary *Elvis on Tour,* the year 1972 witnessed several other career highlights. Elvis made entertainment history in June 1972 with his four-show engagement at Madison Square Garden. He was the first performer to sell out all of his shows in advance, grossing about $730,000. A total of 80,000 people, including Bob Dylan, Art Garfunkel, John Lennon, and George Harrison, attended the performances. David Bowie came to the show in full Ziggy Stardust costume, which he later admitted was a mistake. RCA recorded all four shows for a possible album. The June 10 performance was chosen, and RCA had the album produced, pressed, and in the stores less than two weeks later.

In addition, *Disc* magazine named him Top Male Singer in February. He also set attendance records at various stadiums and arenas. During this year, Elvis met Linda Thompson with whom he experienced his final long-lasting relationship.

# IN THE NEWS IN 1972

- President Nixon visits Chairman Mao in China.

- Governor George Wallace is shot in Maryland while campaigning for president. He survives but is paralyzed.

- The last U.S. ground troops leave Vietnam.

1972 Munich Olympics

- Palestinian terrorists murder 11 Israeli athletes at the Munich Olympics.

- Nixon is re-elected president in a landslide victory.

- A June break-in at the Democratic Headquarters in the Watergate Hotel is the beginning of the end for Nixon's presidency.

# Graceland

*Elvis purchased Graceland in March 1957. It is located at 3764 Elvis Presley Boulevard in Memphis, Tennessee.*

The home most associated with Elvis Presley is Graceland, which he purchased in March 1957 for slightly more than $100,000. The house is located on 13.8 acres of land on the outskirts of Memphis, which afforded the Presley family some much needed privacy. Over the years, Elvis made several additions and improvements to Graceland until the mansion consisted of 23 rooms, and the grounds included the Trophy Room and Meditation Garden, as well as a carport, bath house, and racquetball court. It could be argued that Graceland was both a sanctuary and a prison to Elvis, protecting him from the ravages of fame but also isolating him from the real world. He died at home on August 16, 1977.

Graceland was opened to the public in 1982 and became a part of the Elvis myth. It was placed on the National Register of Historic Places in 1991 and was named a National Historic Landmark in 2006. Each year, between 600,000 and 650,000 visitors come through the Music Gate to view the sights at Graceland.

## THE KING IS DEAD
## *Long Live the King*

### HEADLINES: AUGUST 17, 1977

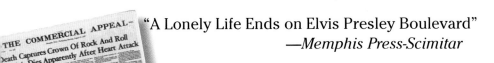

"A Lonely Life Ends on Elvis Presley Boulevard"
—*Memphis Press-Scimitar*

"Death Captures Crown Of Rock And Roll"
—*The Commercial Appeal*

"The King Is Dead"
—*Tupelo Daily Journal*

"All Roads Lead to Memphis"
—*Evening Standard (London)*

"Last Stop on the Mystery Train"
—*Time* magazine

"L'adieu a Elvis"
—*France-Soir*

"Elvis Has Left the Building"
—*Stereo Review*

# "Elvis, I fondle your hair in my dreams."

—*Graffiti on the wall around Graceland*

# Memphis

*Elvis is on Beale Street in Memphis. The Malco Theater was a favorite haunt of Elvis in the 1960s, when he would rent the theater after hours to watch movies with his friends.*

In September 1948, the Presleys moved to Memphis, because the city promised better job opportunities for Gladys and Vernon. In Memphis, Elvis was exposed to gospel, rhythm-and-blues, and country music, which he would later integrate to form his unique sound. Music became the path that would lead Elvis and his family to a better life, and Memphis was an integral part of that. Elvis remained loyal to Memphis throughout his life and career, and though he owned houses in California, Memphis was his home.

One year after his death, many fans journeyed to Memphis to stand in front of Graceland. They lit candles by the Music Gate to pay their respects. The year after that, a few fan clubs organized several events in mid-August as a way to commemorate Elvis Presley's life and music. This was the beginning of Elvis Week. In 1980, Bill Burk, a reporter for the *Memphis Press-Scimitar* and who had often interviewed Elvis, offered to help schedule the fan club events to avoid conflicts. When Graceland opened to the public in 1982, the operations manager for the estate declared that from that year onward, the week would be known as Elvis Presley International Tribute Week. Over the years, the city has taken advantage of Graceland and Elvis Week to promote its history, musical heritage, and rich Southern culture.

For fans around the world, Memphis is Elvis City. For anyone with even a passing interest in 20th-century popular music, Memphis and Graceland are essential places to visit and absorb the history.

**"I only really feel at home in Memphis, at my own Graceland mansion. A man gets lonesome for the things that are familiar to him. I know I do."**

*—Elvis, speaking of his beloved home*

# RETURN TO SENDER:

## *The Elvis Stamp*

Issued by the U.S. Postal Service in 1993 on Elvis's birthday, January 8, the Elvis stamp became a popular and inexpensive piece of memorabilia.

In an ingenius marketing move, the Post Office asked the public to vote on the final stamp design. A ballot was issued that featured two illustrations of the singer—one depicting a rock 'n' roll Elvis and the other, a Vegas Elvis. After a voting period of several months, the rock 'n' roll Elvis won.

Not everyone was delighted with the stamp, however. Consumer-advocate Ralph Nader remarked that the Postal Service was wasteful because it spent $300,000 to promote the stamp. According to Nader, "To break even, they would have to sell more than one million stamps to collectors who do not then use them." Nader, however, underestimated the legendary singer's significance. A few months later, the Postal Service announced it had made a record $31 million.

As of 2006, the Elvis stamp remains the most popular stamp ever produced.

# 30 #1 Hits

To commemorate the 25th anniversary of Elvis's death, RCA released a compilation of his number-one records. *Elvis: 30 #1 Hits* rocketed to number one when it debuted, selling 500,000 copies in its first week of release. Debuting an album in the top spot on the U.S. charts was an accomplishment Elvis had not managed while he was alive. *30 #1 Hits* opened at number one in 16 other countries, including Canada, France, the United Kingdom, Argentina, and the United Arab Emirates.

Arranged in chronological order, the compilation of hits covered Elvis's entire career at RCA—from "Heartbreak Hotel" in 1956 to "Way Down" in 1977. All songs reached number one on the charts at the time of their original release, either in the United States or the United Kingdom. This fact counters the accusations of some critics who claim Elvis's music in the latter part of his career was in decline. After years of undeserved jokes, misunderstandings, and unsubstantiated criticisms aimed at Elvis, the world needed to be reminded of his music.

# "Before anyone did anything, Elvis did everything."

*— Marketing campaign for* Elvis: 30 #1 Hits

1. Heartbreak Hotel
2. Don't Be Cruel
3. Hound Dog
4. Love Me Tender
5. Too Much
6. All Shook Up
7. Teddy Bear,
   (Let Me Be Your)
8. Jailhouse Rock
9. Don't
10. Hard Headed Woman
11.  One Night
12. A Fool Such As I
    (Now and Then There's)
13. A Big Hunk O' Love
14. Stuck on You
15. It's Now or Never
16. Are You Lonesome
    Tonight?
17. Wooden Heart
18. Surrender
19. His Latest Flame
    (Marie's the Name)
20. Can't Help Falling In
    Love
21. Good Luck Charm
22. She's Not You
23. Return to Sender
24. Devil in Disguise,
    (You're The)
25. Crying in the Chapel
26. In the Ghetto
27. Suspicious Minds
28. The Wonder of You
29. Burning Love
30. Way Down
31. A Little Less
    Conversation
    (radio edit remix,
    bonus track)

# ESSENTIAL MYTH
## Elvis Is Alive

*This Hollywood publicity photo is from the 1956 film,* Love Me Tender.

The most annoying question you can ask any Elvis fan is: "Is Elvis alive?" It is an aspect of the Elvis myth that still lingers, generally through jokes by late-night comedians or non-fans.

Rumors began to stir in 1979 that Elvis was still alive when Gail Brewer-Giorgio wrote *Orion,* a novel in which the Presley-like protagonist arranges his own death in order to find peace and privacy. Then in 1981, a book by Steven C. Chanzes claimed that a terminally ill impersonator had been interred at Graceland instead of the real Elvis. Both books flopped, and the rumors quickly faded. In 1987, Brewer-Giorgio revived the rumors with her self-published *The Most Incredible Elvis Presley Story Ever Told,* in which she claimed *Orion* failed because it had been squelched by important Presley people. Her book was republished the following year as *Is Elvis Alive?* The resulting publicity started a full-scale media blitz, culminating in Elvis sightings at fast-food restaurants, cheap motels, and even at Chernobyl, Russia, shortly after the nuclear disaster.

Yet, as tasteless as this tired, old rumor has become, it is a symbol of our collective desire to keep Elvis's name and music alive, not merely by the fans, but by all of us. He embodied so much that our culture admires—an indigenous popular art form, the American Dream, a working class hero, rebellious youth—that we refuse to lay him to rest. Elvis is indeed alive . . . in the latest pop music sensation who generates a controversy, in every working class kid who makes it big, and in every girl who screams hysterically at the wild-eyed boy in the rock 'n' roll band.

---

*"Elvis was the King of Rock 'n' Roll because he was the embodiment of its sins and virtues, grand and vulgar, rude and elegant, powerful and frustrated, absurdly simple and awesomely complex. He was the King . . . in our hearts, which is the place where the music really comes to life. And just as Rock 'n' Roll will stand as long as our hearts beat, he will always be our king."*

—*Dave Marsh, pop music critic and historian*

## ESSENTIAL BOOKS
# *Elvis as a Cultural Phenomenon*

*Dead Elvis: A Chronicle of a Cultural Obsession* by Greil Marcus

*The Elvis Atlas: A Journey Through Elvis Presley's America* by Michael Gray and Roger Osborne

*Elvis for Beginners* by Jill Pearlman

*Elvis Is Everywhere: Photographs by Rowland Scherman* edited by Mark Pollard

*Elvis: His Life from A to Z* by Fred L. Worth and Steve D. Tamerius

*Dear Elvis: Graffiti from Graceland* by Daniel Wright

## ESSENTIAL BIOGRAPHIES

*Early Elvis: The Tupelo Years, The Humes Years, and The Sun Years* by Bill E. Burk

*All Shook Up: Elvis Day-by-Day, 1954–1977* by Lee Cotten

*Elvis and Gladys* by Elaine Dundy

*When Elvis Died* by Neal & Janice Gregory

*Last Train to Memphis* and *Careless Love* by Peter Guralnik